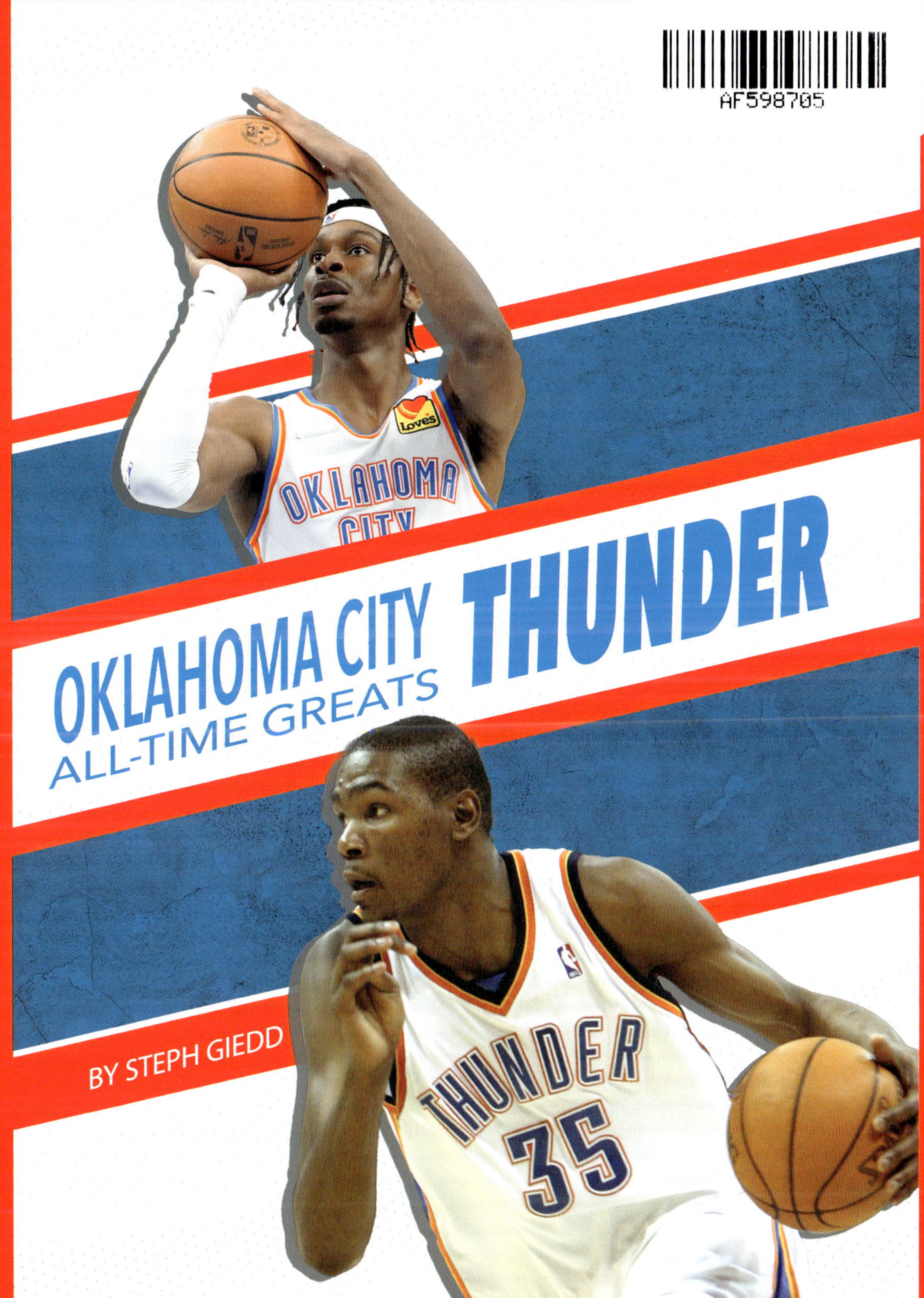
AF598705
OKLAHOMA CITY
OKLAHOMA CITY
THUNDER
ALL-TIME GREATS
BY STEPH GIEDD
THUNDER
35

Book design by Jake Slavik
Cover design by Jake Slavik

Photographs ©: Sue Ogrocki/AP Images, cover (top), cover (bottom), 1 (top), 1 (bottom), 19; AP Images, 4, 7; Steve Pyle/AP Images, 8; Gary Stewart/AP Images, 10; Kirby Lee/AP Images, 13; Alex Brandon/AP Images, 15; Morry Gash/AP Images, 16; Nick Wass/AP Images, 21

Press Box Books, an imprint of Press Room Editions.

ISBN
978-1-63494-666-7 (library bound)
978-1-63494-690-2 (paperback)
978-1-63494-737-4 (epub)
978-1-63494-714-5 (hosted ebook)

Library of Congress Control Number: 2022919280

Distributed by North Star Editions, Inc.
2297 Waters Drive
Mendota Heights, MN 55120
www.northstareditions.com

Printed in the United States of America
082023

ABOUT THE AUTHOR

Steph Giedd is a former high school English teacher turned sports editor. Originally from southern Iowa, Steph now lives in Minneapolis, Minnesota, with her husband, daughter, and pets.

TABLE OF CONTENTS

WILKENS
19
CELTICS
12
Seattle
CELTICS
10

CHAPTER 1
SEEING SEATTLE

The original home of the Thunder was not Oklahoma City. The team actually began its NBA journey as the Seattle SuperSonics in 1967–68.

The Sonics' first standout was veteran point guard **Lenny Wilkens**. He was one of the best passers of his era. In 1969–70, Wilkens led the NBA with an average of 9.1 assists per game. Though Seattle struggled, Wilkens made three All-Star teams in four years with the team.

Spencer Haywood joined the team in 1970. The forward averaged a double-double in each of his first four seasons with the team. The 6'8", 225-pound Haywood then helped the Sonics earn their first playoff berth in 1975.

The SuperSonics hit new heights in 1979. Seattle won its first NBA title. The star-studded Sonics team dominated the Washington Bullets. Seattle won the Finals in five games. Shooting guard **Fred Brown** was a big part of the team's success. And the elite scorer played his entire 13-year career in Seattle.

COACH WILKENS

Lenny Wilkens was a great player when he was traded to Seattle in 1968. A year later, Wilkens was named head coach while still playing. He left in 1972 but returned to coach from 1977 to 1985. Wilkens left as an NBA champion and the franchise's all-time leader in coaching wins.

Cavaliers
HAYWOOD
24

SONICS
24
JOHNSON
24

However, Brown was overshadowed during the 1979 Finals by **Dennis Johnson**. The guard recorded 22.6 points, 6.0 assists, and 2.2 steals per game in the Finals. Johnson was named the Finals Most Valuable Player (MVP).

Seattle selected **Jack Sikma** in the 1977 NBA Draft. The center could defend the paint. And he was a monster on the glass.

However, the main focus of the Sonics' championship squad was **Gus Williams**. "The Wizard" led the team in points. And the guard was a tricky passer. The SuperSonics made the playoffs every season with this core.

STAT SPOTLIGHT

CAREER REBOUNDS

THUNDER TEAM RECORD

Jack Sikma: 7,729

ELLIS
3
SONICS
3

CHAPTER 2

SUCCESS OUT WEST

The SuperSonics continued to make the playoffs in the 1980s. They acquired more talented players too. But they couldn't make a championship run.

Seattle traded for **Dale Ellis** in 1986. He broke out as a key player that year and was voted the NBA's Most Improved Player. He led the SuperSonics in scoring for four seasons straight.

One of Seattle's draft picks was **Nate McMillan** in 1986. His stats weren't flashy. But the point guard was a great defender. He led the NBA in steals in 1993–94 while coming off the bench.

McMillan backed up guard **Gary Payton**. "The Glove" was a lockdown defender. But he was also an offensive leader. Payton partnered with forward **Shawn Kemp** in the early 1990s. Kemp was a powerful dunker. And he was at his best close to the hoop. These two stars were key in Seattle's run to the NBA Finals in 1996.

Payton was voted Defensive Player of the Year that season. Seattle met the powerhouse Chicago Bulls in the Finals. Payton caused Bulls superstar Michael Jordan to have two of his

STAT SPOTLIGHT

CAREER GAMES PLAYED

THUNDER TEAM RECORD

Gary Payton: 999

SEATTLE
20
PAYTON
20

worst playoff games. But the SuperSonics ended up losing the series.

Another key piece to the Finals run was **Detlef Schrempf**. The forward mostly came off the bench early in his career. But he was a consistent starter in six seasons with Seattle.

Rashard Lewis was another forward who made an impact after he was drafted in 1998. He made more than 38 percent of his threes with the Sonics.

BRING THE THUNDER

The SuperSonics moved to Oklahoma after the 2007–08 season. With the new location, they needed a new name. Fans could vote on options based on what the city is known for: Thunder, Bison, Wind, Energy, Marshalls, and Barons. Thunder was chosen because of the area's brutal thunderstorms.

Sharpshooter **Ray Allen** was in Seattle fewer than five seasons. But the guard is still

seen as one of the team's greatest scorers. He averaged 24.6 points per game with the Sonics. But there was not much success during the final seasons in Seattle. Ownership decided to move the team to Oklahoma City.

WESTBROOK
0
OKLAHOMA CITY
0

CHAPTER 3
THE THUNDER ROLLS

It only took the Thunder one season to make the playoffs after moving from Seattle. They continued to improve quickly.

Forward **Kevin Durant** and point guard **Russell Westbrook** were the dynamic duo of the early Oklahoma years. The two led the team to the 2012 NBA Finals, along with **James Harden**.

STAT SPOTLIGHT

CAREER POINTS

THUNDER TEAM RECORD

Russell Westbrook: 18,859

Durant joined the team when it was still in Seattle. His skills were one of a kind for his size. The tall forward played like a guard. He won the MVP award in 2013–14. In his nine seasons with the team, Durant established himself as one of the greatest players in NBA history.

After Durant left in 2016, Westbrook was the team's main star. He won the scoring title and MVP in 2016–17. It was the first of three straight years in which he averaged a triple-double.

Harden played in Oklahoma City from 2009 to 2012. "The Beard" proved to be a great shooter and an even better ball handler.

TRIPLE-DOUBLES FOR DAYS

In 2016–17, Russell Westbrook averaged 31.6 points, 10.4 assists, and 10.7 rebounds. He was the first player to average a triple-double for a full season since Oscar Robertson in 1961–62. Westbrook set a new record for the most triple-doubles in a season with 42.

Serge Ibaka helped hold down the defense. The 6'10" power forward led the NBA in blocks in 2011–12 and again in 2012–13.

Forward **Paul George** was in Oklahoma City for just two seasons. The rising star helped keep the team competitive after Durant left. George was especially good on defense. He led the league with 2.2 steals per game in 2018–19, while still improving offensively. George finished second in the NBA with 28.0 points per game.

The Thunder traded George to the Los Angeles Clippers in 2019. One player they got in the deal was guard **Shai Gilgeous-Alexander**. He became the team's top threat over the next few seasons. The Thunder continued to struggle. But other promising players were soon added. Thunder fans hoped this group had what it took to get the team back to the Finals.

GILGEOUS-
ALEXANDER
2

TIMELINE

1967
1970
1980
1990
2000
2010
2020
2023
LENNY WILKENS
(1968-72)
SPENCER HAYWOOD
(1970-75)
FRED BROWN
(1971-84)
DENNIS JOHNSON
(1976-80)
GUS WILLIAMS
(1977-80, 1981-84)
NATE MCMILLAN
(1986-98)
SHAWN KEMP
(1989-97)
DALE ELLIS
(1986-91, 1997-99)
GARY PAYTON
(1990-2003)
DETLEF SCHREMPF
(1993-99)
RASHARD LEWIS
(1998-2007)
RAY ALLEN
(2003-07)
JAMES HARDEN
(2009-2012)
RUSSELL WESTBROOK
(2008-19)
KEVIN DURANT
(2007-16)
SERGE IBAKA
(2009-16)
PAUL GEORGE
(2017-19)
SHAI GILGEOUS-
ALEXANDER
(2019-)

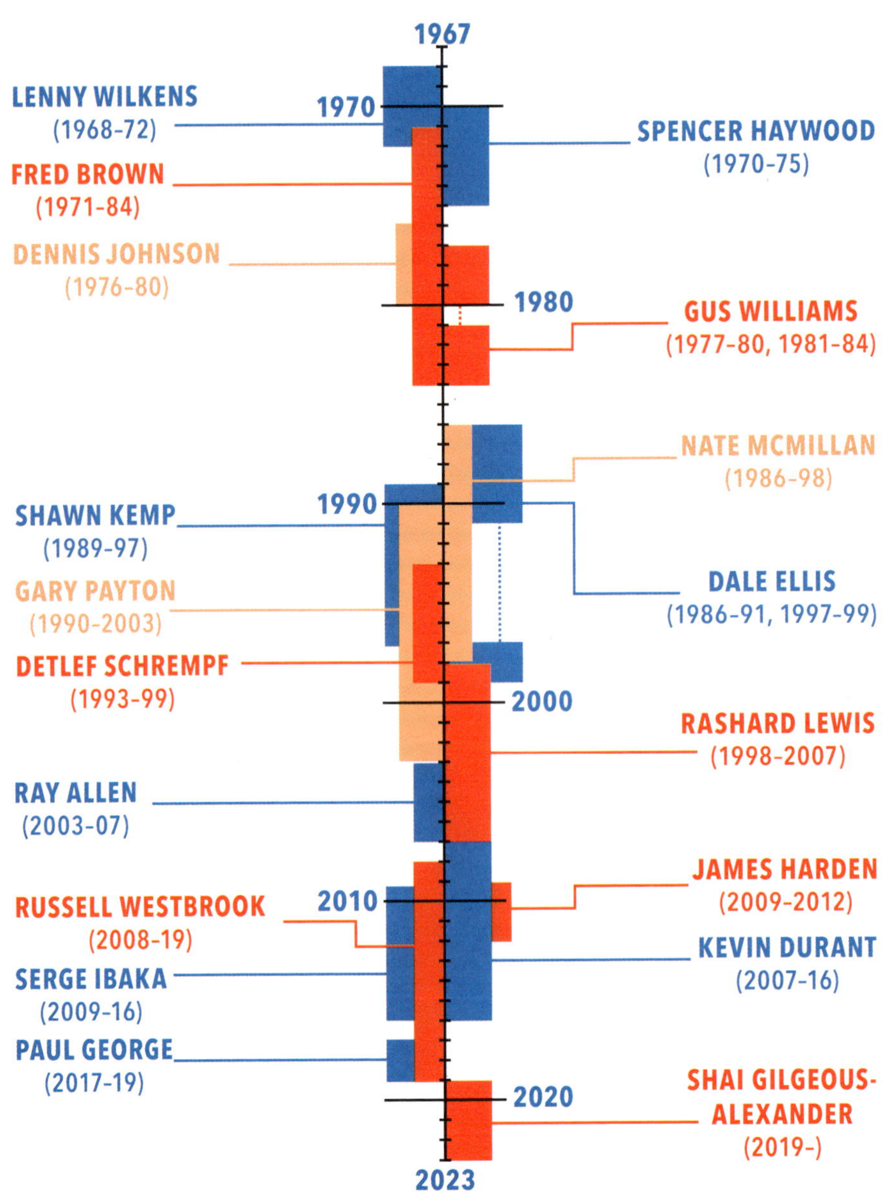

TEAM FACTS

OKLAHOMA CITY THUNDER

Formerly: Seattle SuperSonics (1967–2008)

First season: 1967–68

NBA championships: 1*

Key coaches:

Scott Brooks (2008–09 to 2014–15)
338–207, 39–34 playoffs

George Karl (1991–92 to 1997–98)
384–150, 40–40 playoffs

Lenny Wilkens (1969–1970 to 1971–72, 1977–78 to 1984–85) 478–402, 37–32 playoffs, 1 NBA title

MORE INFORMATION

To learn more about the Oklahoma City Thunder, go to **pressboxbooks.com/AllAccess.**
These links are routinely monitored and updated to provide the most current information available.

**Through 2021–22 season*

GLOSSARY

consistent
Reliable, unchanging.

draft
An event that allows teams to choose new players coming into the league.

elite
The best of the best.

lockdown
Capable of shutting down the best offensive players.

paint
Another term for the lane, the area between the basket and the free throw line.

sharpshooter
A player who is known for making many shots.

triple-double
A game in which a player has double-digit numbers in three categories.

INDEX